Long, Long ago

In Bethlehem ...

Long, Long ago
In Bethlehem

The Birth of Jesus

Told by Carine Mackenzie

Illustrated by Fred Apps

Published by Christian Focus Publications

© 1999 Christian Focus Publications Ltd
Geanies House, Fearn,
Tain, Ross-shire IV20 1TW

Illustrations by Fred Apps
Written by Carine Mackenzie
ISBN 1-85792-386 3

Long, long ago, two thousand years ago something very exciting happened.

A baby boy was born. Why was this exciting? What was special about this little baby? Well, this little baby was and is the Son of God and his name is Jesus Christ. All over the world the arrival of the year 2000 is being celebrated in a big way because two thousand years ago God sent his son to earth as a baby boy and they gave him the name, Jesus.

The birth of the Lord Jesus Christ, the Son of God is the amazing event that took place 2,000 years ago. We do not know the exact date but when calendars were invented the year of Jesus Christ's birth was used as the starting point.

Do not forget Jesus in all the excitement of the new millennium. Read all about his remarkable birth and wonder at the love of God who gave his only Son that whoever believes on him should not perish but will have eternal life.

When the millennium is over and the celebrations are just memories in the past read again this amazing story. It may be two thousand years old but it is just as exciting as the day that it happened...

...Long, long ago in Bethlehem.

This book was presented to:

....

With much love from:

....

On:

....

May the LORD bless you and keep you.
May the LORD make his face shine upon you and be gracious to you.
May the LORD turn his face towards you and give you peace.
Numbers Chapter 6 Verses 24-26.

Mary, was a young Jewish woman who lived in the village of Nazareth in the land of Israel.

One day, an angel came to Mary and gave her an amazing piece of news.

'You are going to have a baby boy. You will call his name Jesus.'

'How can that be?' she asked.

'The baby is the Son of God. You will have this child by the special power of the Holy Spirit.'

Mary was engaged to Joseph. When he heard Mary was expecting a baby, he was alarmed and unhappy. God sent Joseph a message in a dream.

An angel said, 'Do not be afraid to take Mary as your wife. The child she is expecting is the Son of God. When the baby is born, you shall call his name Jesus (which means Saviour) for he shall save his people from their sins.'
So Joseph was happy to marry Mary.

An order came from the ruler of the land that everyone had to go to their home town to be counted. Joseph and Mary had to travel from Nazareth to Bethlehem - even although Mary's baby was due to be born soon.

When they reached Bethlehem the whole town was busy. They could find no room at the inn. They had to find shelter where the animals were fed.

For to us a child is born,
to us a son is given,
and the government
shall be on his shoulders.
And he will be called
Wonderful Counsellor,
Mighty God,
Everlasting Father,
Prince of Peace.
Of the increase of his
government and peace
there will be no end.
Isaiah 9: 6-7

But you,
Bethlehem,
though you are small
among the clans of
Judah,
out of you will come
for me one who will
be ruler over Israel ...

Micah 5:2

When the baby was born, Mary wrapped him up carefully and laid him in the manger for a cot. A manger was normally used for holding straw and food that the sheep would eat. So the manger and the straw were made into a bed for baby Jesus.

In the country-side nearby, shepherds watched over their sheep. Suddenly their eyes were dazzled as an angel appeared in the sky. They were afraid. 'Don't be afraid,' the angel said. 'I bring good news. Today a Saviour has been born in Bethlehem. Go now you will find the baby in a manger.' Suddenly there was a crowd of angels, each praising God saying, 'Glory to God in the highest. Peace and good will to all people.'

The shepherds hurried to Bethlehem and found Mary and Joseph, and the baby lying in the manger. The shepherds told everyone that they met the amazing news. Then they returned to their work, praising and worshipping God.

W hen the baby was eight days old he was given the name Jesus, just as the angel had told Joseph and Mary. Mary and Joseph took the young baby Jesus to the temple to present him to the Lord and to offer a sacrifice as the law of God required.

In the temple they met a good, old, man called Simeon. God had given Simeon a special promise that he would not die until he had seen Jesus Christ, the promised Saviour.

When Simeon saw Mary and Joseph with the baby he knew that at last he was looking at the Saviour. He took baby Jesus in his arms and praised the Lord.

An old lady called Anna then met the baby Jesus. Anna spent all her time praying in the temple.

She was so thankful to God that she had actually seen the promised Saviour, Jesus Christ. She passed on the good news to others.

Magi from the east came
to Jerusalem and asked,
'Where is the one who has
been born king of the Jews?
We saw his star in the
east and have come to
worship him.'

Matthew 2:1-2

All the ends
of the earth
will see
the salvation
of our God.

Isaiah 52:10

Wise men from the East saw a special star and knew that the King of the Jews had been born. They travelled to King Herod's Palace in Jerusalem to find out more.

Herod asked where this king would be born.

'... In Bethlehem,' his religious leaders replied.

Herod said to the Wise men, 'Tell me when you have found this child. I will worship him too.' But Herod was a liar. He wanted to kill the young child, Jesus, instead.

When they left King Herod, the wise men were guided by a special star, right to the house where Jesus was. They came into the house and fell down before the young child Jesus and worshipped him. They knew he was the Son of God and gave him presents of gold, frankincense and myrrh.

They did not go back to tell King Herod where Jesus was, because God warned them in a dream that Herod planned to kill Jesus. The wise men went home another way.

When Israel was a child, I loved him, and out of Egypt I called my son.

Hosea 11:1

So he got up, took the child
and his mother during the
night and left for Egypt,
where he stayed until the
death of Herod. And so was
fullfilled what the Lord had
said through the prophet:
'Out of Egypt
I called my son.'

Matthew 2:14-15

The angel of the Lord then spoke to Joseph in a dream. 'Take young Jesus and Mary away from here. Go to Egypt. Stay there until I tell you it is safe to return. King Herod wants to destroy the young child.'

So when it was dark Joseph, Mary and Jesus left their home and travelled to the land of Egypt.

After Herod died an angel spoke to Joseph in another dream.

'Take the young child and his mother back to Israel. The people who wanted to kill Jesus are dead. It is safe to go back.'

Joseph took Mary and Jesus back to Israel and they settled in the village of Nazareth.

Jesus grew up there - he was a wise and good boy who lived in a way that was pleasing to God, his heavenly Father.

We should remember on every day of the year the wonderful fact that Jesus was born. The angels told the shepherds that the new born baby was the Saviour of the world – the good news was for all people – you as well.

God has sent his Son to the world to be the Saviour because he loves us so much.

Our response should be to believe in the Saviour and to obey his word.

But he was
pierced for
our sins.
He was
crushed for
our sins
By his wounds we are
healed.

Isaiah

53:5

Seek the Lord
while he may be found
call on him
while he is near.

Isaiah 55:6

But the story doesn't end in Bethlehem.
Jesus' story continues
to other towns and other places.
In another town, many years later,
he died on a cross.
Jesus, the Son of God died
so that you could live.
Think for a minute about what this means.
It was because of your sins that Jesus died.
It was because of your sins
that Jesus had to live in a world of sin.
It was because of your sins
that he was born in a stable,
long, long ago in Bethlehem.
Thank Jesus for his love.
Thank him for his beautiful gift
of forgiveness.
Thank him for the price he has paid...
the price he has paid for you.